P9-BIA-445

KATHLEEN KRULL

illustrated by
CARLYN BECCIA

LOUISA MAY'S BATTLE

How the CIVIL WAR Led to *LITTLE WOMEN*

WALKER BOOKS FOR YOUNG READERS
AN IMPRINT OF BLOOMSBURY
NEW YORK   LONDON   NEW DELHI   SYDNEY

Welcome to a future Little Woman,
Ruth Lenore Armour, April 13, 2012 —K. K.

In memory of John Beccia Sr.;
Christmas won't be Christmas without you —C. B.

Text copyright © 2013 by Kathleen Krull
Illustrations copyright © 2013 by Carlyn Beccia
All rights reserved. No part of this book may be reproduced or transmitted in any form
or by any means, electronic or mechanical, including photocopying, recording, or by any
information storage and retrieval system, without permission in writing from the publisher.

First published in the United States of America in March 2013
by Walker Books for Young Readers, an imprint of Bloomsbury Publishing, Inc.
www.bloomsburykids.com

For information about permission to reproduce selections from this book, write to
Permissions, Walker BFYR, 175 Fifth Avenue, New York, New York 10010

Library of Congress Cataloging-in-Publication Data
Krull, Kathleen.
Louisa May's Battle : how the Civil War led to Little Women / by Kathleen Krull;
illustrated by Carlyn Beccia.
p.   cm.
ISBN 978-0-8027-9668-4 (hardcover) • ISBN 978-0-8027-9669-1 (reinforced)
1. Alcott, Louisa May, 1832–1888—Juvenile literature. 2. Authors, American—19th century—
Biography—Juvenile literature. 3. Nurses—United States—Biography—Juvenile literature.
4. United States—History—Civil War, 1861–1865—Juvenile literature.
I. Beccia, Carlyn, ill. II. Title.
PS1018.K78 2013   813'.4—dc23 [B]   2012016633

Art created with Corel Painter digital oils on gessoed canvas
Typeset in Horley Old Style
Book design by Nicole Gastonguay

Printed in China by C&C Offset Printing Co., Ltd., Shenzhen, Guangdong
2 4 6 8 10 9 7 5 3 1 (hardcover)
2 4 6 8 10 9 7 5 3 1 (reinforced)

All papers used by Bloomsbury Publishing, Inc., are natural, recyclable products
made from wood grown in well-managed forests. The manufacturing processes
conform to the environmental regulations of the country of origin.

"I'll be rich and famous and happy before I die, see if I won't!"
—LOUISA MAY ALCOTT, fifteen years old

*D*uring the Civil War (1861–1865), the army saw its soldiers, boys and men, dying at a shocking pace. It grew desperate for more doctors and nurses—desperate enough to allow women to serve.

For a woman to work outside the home was rare; it was considered indecent and unhealthy. Women doctors were almost unheard of. But perhaps a woman could be a nurse, if she was at least thirty, "very plain," unmarried, strong, with two letters about her good character.

Many people, even many doctors, disapproved. Most nurses at that time were men, like the famous poet Walt Whitman. But eventually several thousand women would serve as Civil War army nurses.

On her thirtieth birthday, a not-very-successful writer applied to be one of them. Her name was Louisa May Alcott.

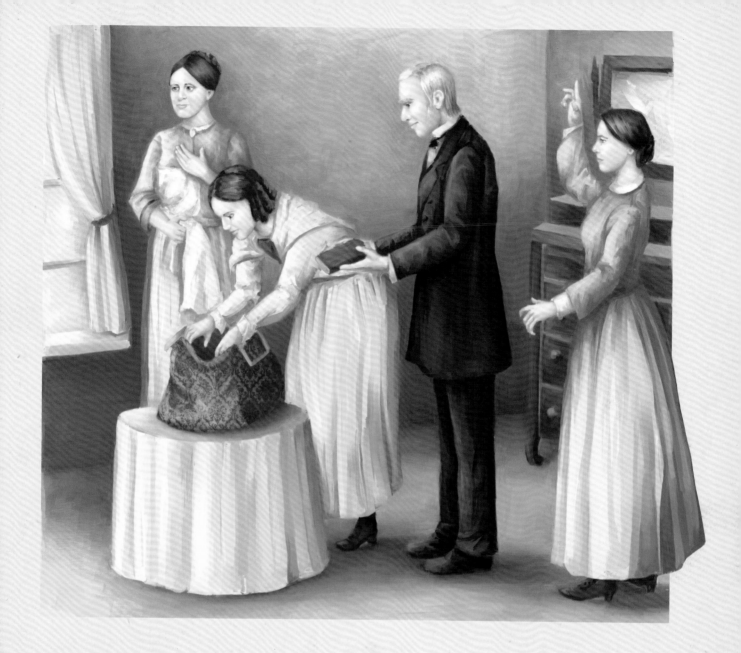

"I long to be a man," Louisa May Alcott scribbled one day, "but as I can't fight, I will content myself with working for those who can." Coming from a family that was part of the Underground Railroad to shelter runaway slaves, she burned to help the war effort.

Four years earlier, she had nursed her beloved sister Elizabeth, stricken with scarlet fever, through her final days. She met the army's rules for nurses, had always been as strong as a horse, and considered herself plain indeed . . . except for her hair, a rich brown lushness that fell all the way to her feet when not pinned up.

Her parents and sisters swarmed, helping her pack. They would miss her dreadfully—for years she had kept the family going with money from sewing, teaching, and writing—but this adventure was sure to make them prouder of her than ever.

On December 12, 1862, she set off on her complicated journey from Concord. In her bag were apples, gingerbread, sandwiches, her plainest clothes, paper for writing letters, and books by her favorite author, Charles Dickens.

The free train ticket that was supposed to be waiting for her in Boston wasn't there. Coming from a family "as poor as rats," she had no money to pay for one. She knocked on doors, blushing, tracking down the president of the railroad himself. Boggled by a woman traveling alone, one man after another gave her the runaround.

For some reason her ticket was at the steamboat station—not the train station—and without a moment to spare she was finally on the train to New London, Connecticut.

That night, her seatmate helped her get to a ship called *City of Boston* for an overnight ride to New Jersey. Louisa tried to act as though she was used to being on a boat, but in fact she was terrified. Surely it would blow up or sink.

Her naps, full of nightmares, were interrupted by things dropping off a shelf. Each time she would jump up in alarm and hit her head on the top of her berth. When the sun appeared over Long Island Sound, she was wide-awake on deck.

Back on another train through Philadelphia and Baltimore, she started writing her first letter home—all about the other passengers. Nearing Washington, the train jolted to a stop, knocking everyone out of their seats and requiring repairs.

It was dark when she finally got to the Georgetown area of Washington, five hundred miles from where she had started. A kind stranger stopped her from getting in the wrong carriage, helped her find the right one, and even gave her a little tour. He pointed out the White House, all lit up, the unfinished Capitol Building without its dome, grand Pennsylvania Avenue—the spaciousness of the city "quite took my breath away."

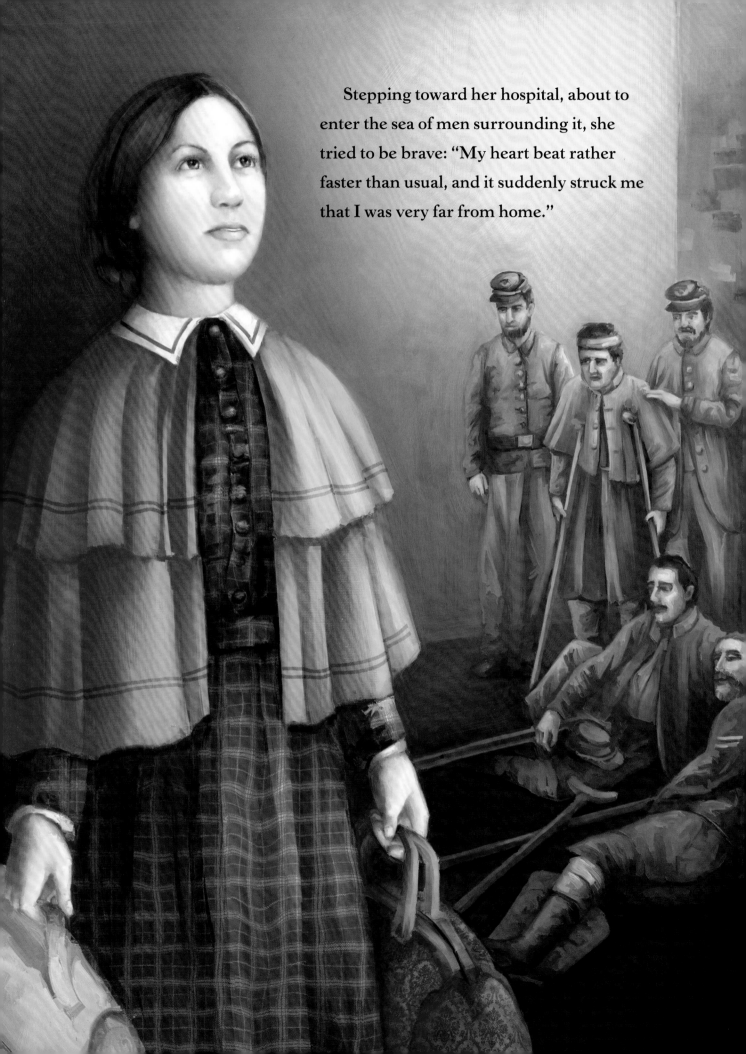

Stepping toward her hospital, about to enter the sea of men surrounding it, she tried to be brave: "My heart beat rather faster than usual, and it suddenly struck me that I was very far from home."

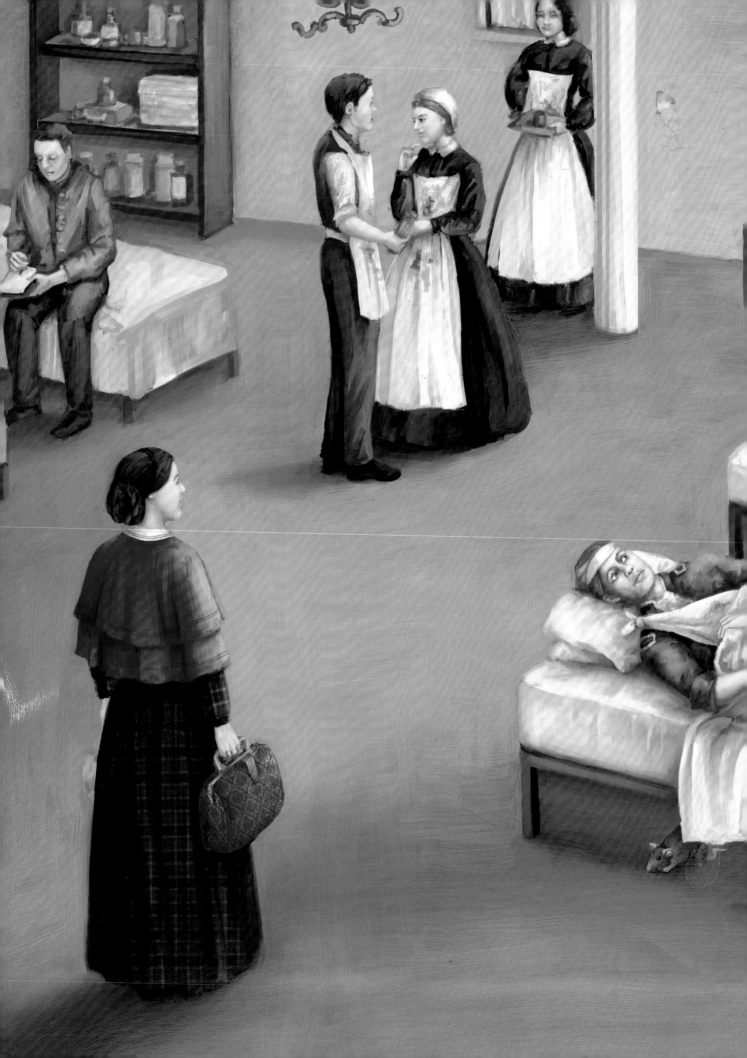

Her "hospital" was actually the old, creaky Union Hotel. It was a breeding ground for germs—overcrowded, damp, dark, airless, its broken windows nailed shut and blocked with curtains to keep out the cold.

In her drafty room, cockroaches scuttled in the walls and rats ruled the closet. Reporting for duty, she was put in charge of a former ballroom. Forty patients were trying to recover from measles, pneumonia, diphtheria, and the dreaded typhoid fever. At first her duties seemed simple enough—"washing faces, serving rations, giving medicine, and sitting in a very hard chair."

Then, on her third day, someone shook her awake at three in the morning. Forty carts were streaming in from the latest battle.

In horror, Louisa watched the carts. As she smelled hundreds of unwashed, sick bodies, she said, "I indulged in a most unpatriotic wish that I was safe at home again."

Then, when she was ordered to bathe the men—not something she'd ever done before—she was almost too shocked to move. But she doused herself with lavender water to distract her nose, rolled up her sleeves, and grabbed sponges and a bar of brown soap.

With her most "businesslike air," she undressed and washed soldiers for the next twelve solid hours. She struggled not to cry in front of any of them, even the wounded boys as young as twelve: "I was there to work, not to wonder or weep."

Over the next few days Louisa got to know her "boys." She brought food to those who could eat, sharing their meals of ancient beef, bread seemingly made of sawdust, and stewed blackberries that looked like "preserved cockroaches." To drink she offered muddy coffee or tea made of three huckleberry leaves in a quart of water.

She helped doctors and learned how to bandage wounds. But she saw her main job as keeping up her patients' spirits. During surgeries she held their hands or brushed their hair. Later, she read to them from Dickens and helped them write letters home. Believing that laughter speeded recovery, she worked at cheering them up. Perhaps most important, she listened to their stories of loss and hope.

Her reward was their heartfelt "Thankee's" and praise: "You are real motherly, ma'am."

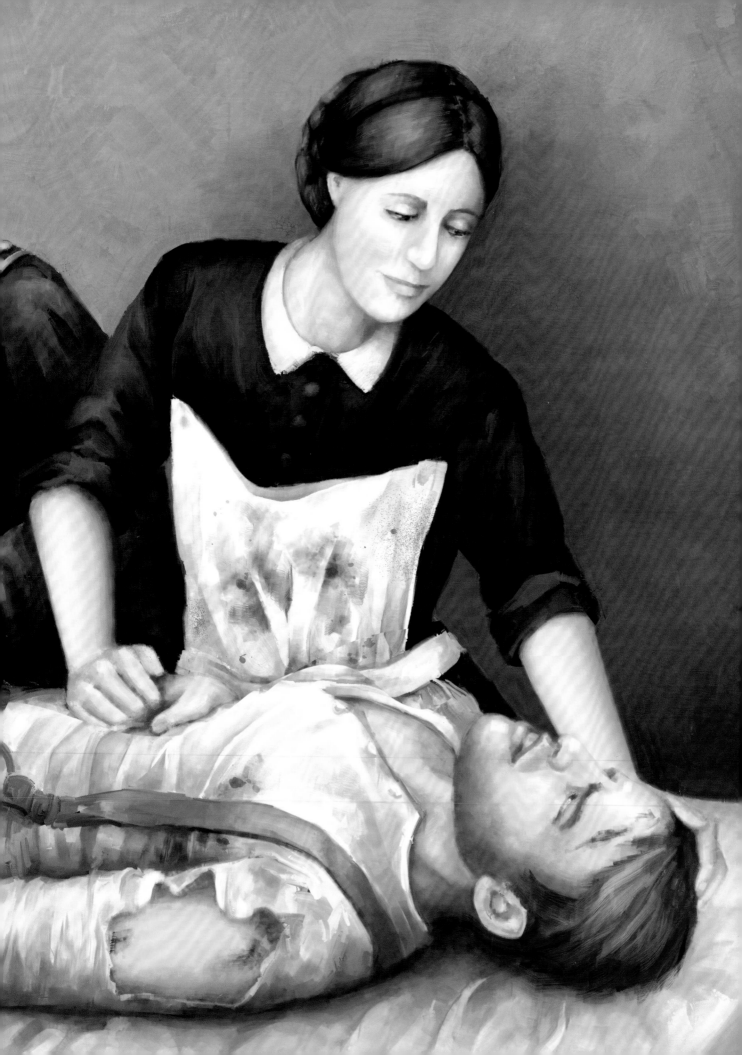

Eventually Louisa took over the night shift in the ballroom. That left mornings free for brisk runs up and down hills, as she tried to stay strong. She could see more wagons taking men into battle, more carts coming back with the wounded. At night she watched her patients sleep, singing lullabies to those who couldn't.

She learned to "cork up" her feelings, to hide them, and she gloried in knowing she was useful. "Though often homesick, heartsick, and worn out, I like it," she wrote.

Any spare minute she had, she wrote home, letters full of snap and bite, using an upside-down teakettle as a desk. She chatted about her soldiers—and also about the chaos at the hospital, or the doctor who had trouble treating his patients as human beings, or the ill treatment some white workers gave black workers.

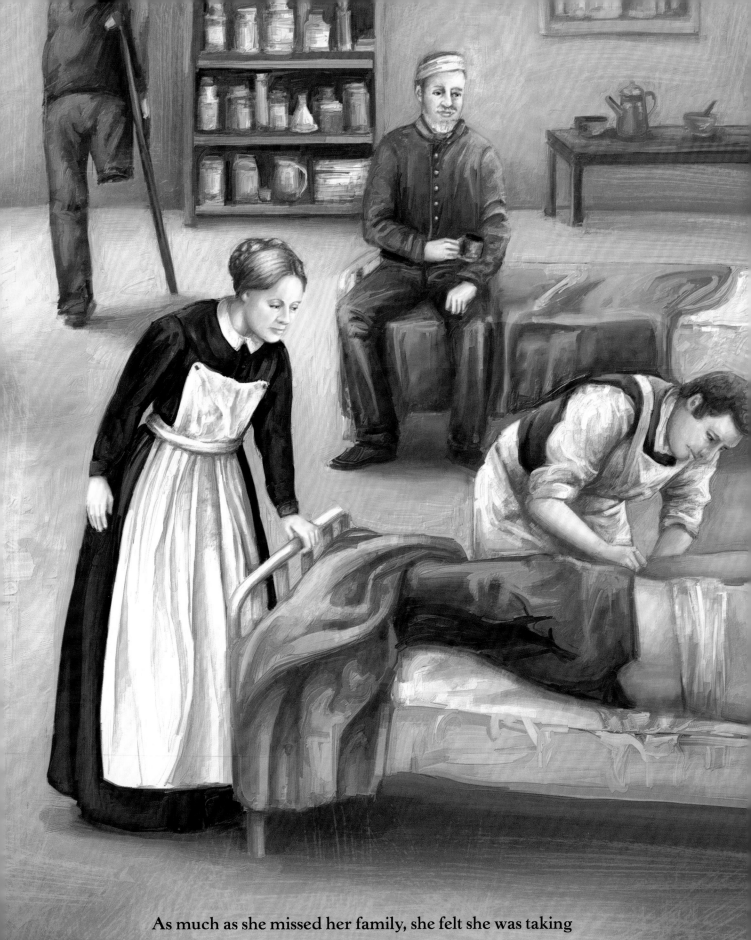

As much as she missed her family, she felt she was taking part in history: "I waited for New Year's Day with more eagerness than I had ever known before."

On January 1, 1863, came the
second part of the Emancipation
Proclamation, freeing slaves in
ten states. Louisa rejoiced: "As the
bells rung midnight, I electrified
my roommate by dancing out of
bed, throwing up the window, and
flapping my handkerchief, with a
feeble cheer" to African Americans
celebrating on the street below.

She had high hopes for justice,
for freed slaves to be "quick to
feel and accept the least token of
the brotherly love which is slowly
teaching the white hand to grasp the
black."

Louisa had never been seriously ill before and didn't worry about catching anything. But three weeks into her job as a nurse, she got a nasty cough. She kept working, though her head was spinning and her temperature shot up. Typhoid fever had struck, and she was sent to bed. She fretted about her "boys" and sat up sewing bandages for them.

But she got worse and worse, and then "the nights were one long fight with weariness and pain." Her letters home stopped suddenly. Stubborn about completing her three-month term, she refused to leave.

Finally her frightened father arrived to take her home, and she was too weak to argue.

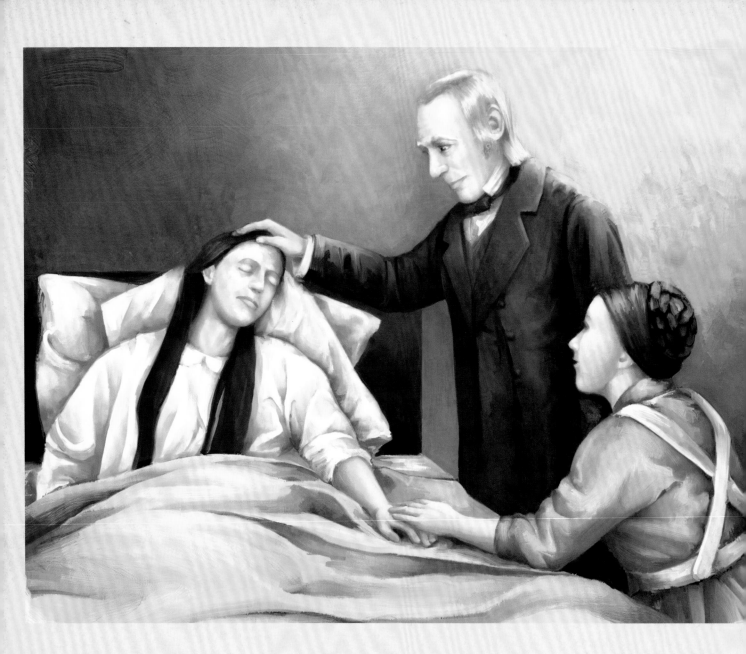

By January 21 she was back with her family, so near death they almost didn't recognize her. Later, she had no memory of her journey home or her first weeks there.

After two solid months in bed, Louisa was never the same, with headaches, exhaustion, nerve pain, and stomach problems. She even lost her hair—"my one beauty"—and was seen taking walks that spring in granny caps and wigs. "A wig outside is better than a loss of wits inside," she tried to joke.

Yet she had no regrets: "All that is best and bravest in the hearts of men and women, comes out in scenes like these; and, though a hospital is a rough school," she had learned so much about human nature—and herself.

Her first worry, once she was up and about, was money. Her army service had earned her a mere ten dollars, so she went back to work, wig in place, to keep the family going.

She'd been publishing books for years, with little praise. Just before she'd left for war, she'd gotten one of her cruelest rejections: "Stick to your teaching; you can't write."

Her response? "I can write, and I'll prove it." She allowed an antislavery newspaper to publish her letters home from the hospital, and soon they were collected as a slender book, *Hospital Sketches*.

Readers were starved for firsthand news of the still-raging war, and here was this account alive with detail of its effect on men's bodies and brains. Reviewers raved about her skill with realism, her large heart, the way she could find humor in the grim setting.

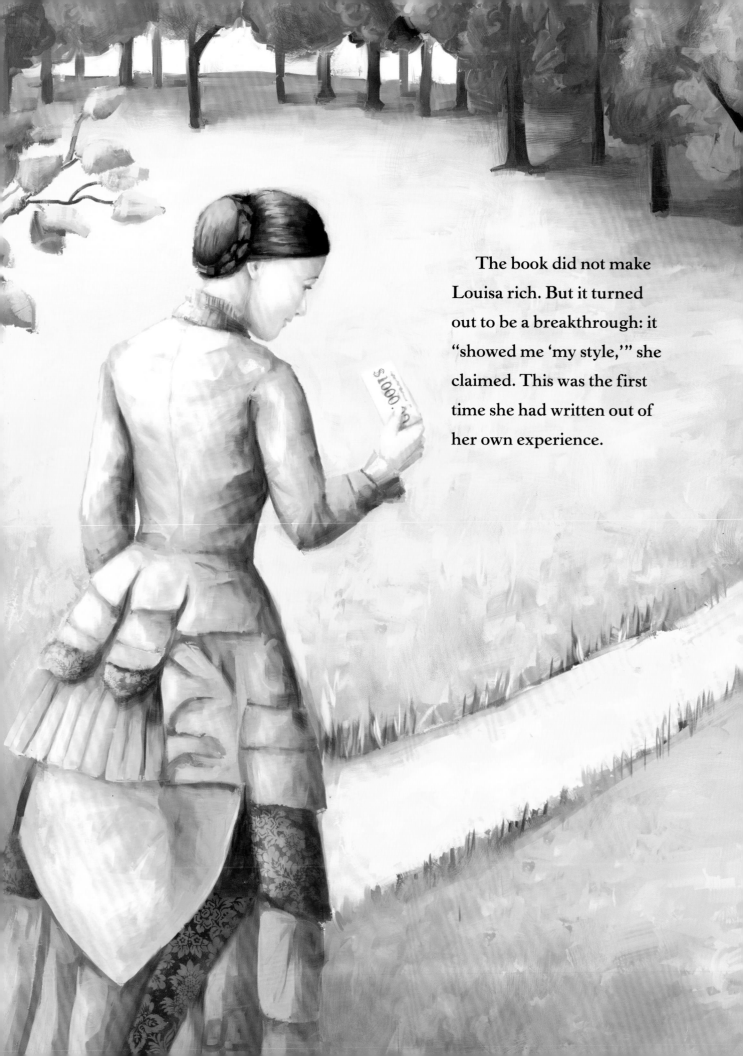

The book did not make Louisa rich. But it turned out to be a breakthrough: it "showed me 'my style,'" she claimed. This was the first time she had written out of her own experience.

She thought about moving to South Carolina as a teacher for newly
freed slaves.

But as she'd once written about a character, "She is too fond of books,
and it has turned her brain." Now editors begged for her writing, and by
October 1863 she was saying, "All my dreams [are] getting fulfilled in a
most amazing way."

By the time the war ended two years later, Louisa was almost
unbelievably prolific, her stories paying off the Alcott bills one by one.

Then she was asked to write "a girls' book." This was just about the last kind of writing she liked to do. She dithered, delayed for a year, then dashed off four hundred pages in ten weeks, stopping for nothing except her daily run.

She stitched together scraps from her childhood, like a quilt, the funny and sad stories of four sisters growing up. To make the novel more immediate and appealing, she set it in the Civil War. While the brilliant but impractical father was ministering to soldiers at the warfront, a wise "Marmee" raised her daughters in poverty.

"Christmas won't be Christmas without any presents" was the novel's first line, said by Jo March—a new kind of heroine: smart, fierce, fearless, a girl with glorious hair.

The line—and Jo and her sisters—was soon to be famous.

Little Women, published in 1868, was one of the first novels set during the Civil War, and it went on to become an enormous bestseller. By the time Louisa was thirty-six, it made all her dreams come true.

During the last years of her life, before her death in 1888, she wrote more and more, earning what would be $2 million a year in today's money. She bought silk dresses for herself and gave lavish gifts to her parents, sisters, nieces, and nephews.

Being a war veteran was the key to all that she accomplished: "My greatest pride is . . . that I had a very small share in the war which put an end to a great wrong."

It was service to her country that made Louisa May Alcott the author of books that would live forever.

❧ WOMEN IN MEDICINE ❧

Besides being an important American writer, Alcott played a part in the early history of women in medicine. The positive response to *Hospital Sketches* inspired other women to volunteer as Civil War nurses.

The woman who had hired her was DOROTHEA DIX, a passionate reformer of prisons and mental hospitals. In 1861 she was appointed superintendent of female nurses at Union Army hospitals and worked without pay throughout the war. Strict (sometimes called "Dragon Dix"), she worked hard to combat the myth that women associated with the army were unladylike or pursuing romance.

HANNAH ROPES, the head nurse at Alcott's hospital, was thrilled with the arrival of "Miss Alcott from Concord—the prospect of a really good nurse, a gentlewoman who can do more than merely keep the patients from falling out of bed." After Ropes and Alcott came down with typhoid—and Ropes died—it was Dix who made sure that Alcott's father came to take her home.

CLARA BARTON was an influential nurse throughout the war, working independently without an official post; in 1881 she became the first president of the new American Red Cross. ELIZABETH BLACKWELL, who in 1849 was the first woman to earn her medical degree, founded her own hospital in New York to treat poor women and children. Unable to find a suitable post in the army, Blackwell spent the war years training women to become nurses. (MARY EDWARDS WALKER was one of the very few women surgeons allowed to serve, as an unpaid volunteer.) The Union Army asked for advice from the pioneering English nurse FLORENCE NIGHTINGALE, but didn't always take it; in 1869 Blackwell and Nightingale cofounded the Women's Medical College in London.

Most of the women in medicine were also active in fighting for equal rights for women—including Alcott, who took to signing her letters "Yours for reform of all kinds."

❦ SOURCES ❦

A NOTE ABOUT DIRECT QUOTES: All Alcott quotes are from *Hospital Sketches*, Alcott's journal, and "Recollections of My Childhood," an article by Alcott.

BOOKS (* especially for young readers)

Anderson, William. *The World of Louisa May Alcott*. New York: HarperCollins, 1995.

Cheever, Susan. *Louisa May Alcott: A Personal Biography*. New York: Simon & Schuster, 2010.

* Kerley, Barbara. *Walt Whitman: Words for America*. New York: Scholastic, 2004.

Matteson, John. *Eden's Outcasts: The Story of Louisa May Alcott and Her Father*. New York: Norton, 2007.

* McDonough, Yona Zeldis. *Louisa: The Life of Louisa May Alcott*. New York: Holt, 2009.

* Meigs, Cornelia. *Invincible Louisa*. Boston: Little, Brown, 1933.

Myerson, Joel, and Daniel Shealy, eds. *The Journals of Louisa May Alcott*. Boston: Little, Brown, 1989.

Rable, George C. *Fredericksburg! Fredericksburg!* Chapel Hill: University of North Carolina Press, 2002.

Re⸺ *⸺lcott: The Woman* ⸺York: Holt, 2009.

* ⸺ *⸺Alcott: Her* ⸺: Bridgewater

Sc⸺ *⸺Front: Hospital* ⸺a. Chapel Hill: ⸺a Press, 2004.

Sh⸺ *⸺ive Alcott*. New ⸺iversity Press, 1988.

W⸺ *⸺urns and Ken* ⸺lustrated History.

WEBSITES

Battle of Fredericksburg, National Park Service: www.nps.gov/frsp/fredhist.htm

Louisa May Alcott: The Woman Behind Little Women, PBS film by Nancy Porter: www.alcottfilm.com

The Louisa May Alcott Society: www.louisamayalcottsociety.org

Louisa May Alcott's *Hospital Sketches*: www.gutenberg.org/etext/3837

Louisa May Alcott's Orchard House: www.louisamayalcott.org

CHILDREN'S BOOKS BY LOUISA MAY ALCOTT

Flower Fables, 1854

The Rose Family: A Fairy Tale, 1864

The Mysterious Key and What It Opened, 1867

Morning-Glories, and Other Stories, 1868

Little Women, published in two volumes: *Meg, Jo, Beth and Amy* in 1868 and *Good Wives* in 1869 (later, it was translated into more than fifty languages and adapted into movies, plays and Broadway musicals, ballets, an opera, Japanese anime, and many other forms)

An Old-Fashioned Girl, 1870

Three Proverb Stories, 1870

Will's Wonder Book, 1870

Little Men: Life at Plumfield with Jo's Boys, 1871

Aunt Jo's Scrap-Bag, 1872–1882

Eight Cousins, 1875

Rose in Bloom, 1876

Under the Lilacs, 1878

Jack and Jill, 1880

Lulu's Library, 1885–1889

Jo's Boys, and How They Turned Out, 1886

A Garland for Girls, 1889

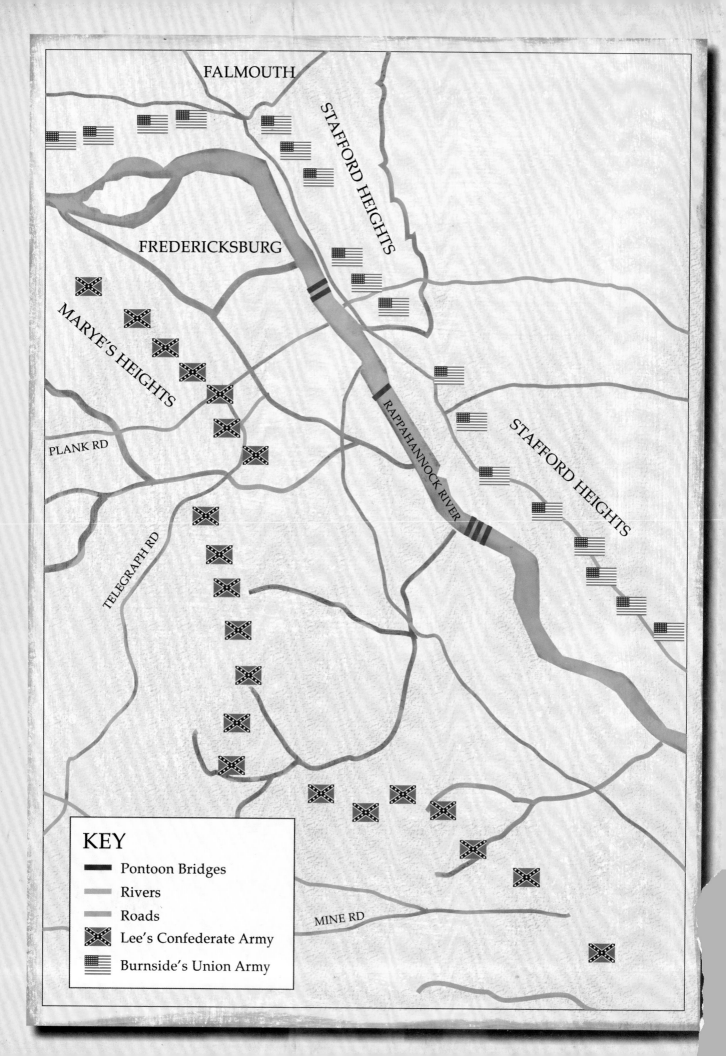

FALMOUTH

STAFFORD HEIGHTS

FREDERICKSBURG

MARYE'S HEIGHTS

PLANK RD

TELEGRAPH RD

RAPPAHANNOCK RIVER

STAFFORD HEIGHTS

MINE RD

KEY

Pontoon Bridges

Rivers

Roads

Lee's Confederate Army

Burnside's Union Army